THE MASTERFUL WRITER SERIES

Masterful Novel Writing: Write Your Novel in 90 Days

Roz Swartz Williams
VISUAL COMMUNICATION CONSULTANT

WWW.LOT21DESIGN.NET

The Masterful Writer Series, Masterful Novel Writing:
Write Your Novel in 90 Days
1st Edition.

Copyright © 2015 by Roz Swartz Williams

For permission requests, contact the publisher
via the information below:

Roz Swartz Williams/Lot:21 Design
rsw@lot21design.net
www.Lot21Design.net

Contents

Foreword

Welcome! Thank you for purchasing this first release of The Masterful Writer Series – created for those who want to build proficiency in the craft of writing in one or many of its various formats. Throughout the Masterful Writer series you'll find helpful guidelines and inspiration for mastering your craft, whether your goal is to make a living as a well-paid corporate writer, find freelance freedom as a writer-entrepreneur, or simply to write well for your personal satisfaction.

The key to masterful writing is developing your ability to create a quality experience for your reader.

Writing may be your passion, but the most important thing to remember is that your writing is not only about you. Writing is a form of speaking. Having conversations. Offering an exchange of information. It's about connecting with others – your reading audience – and providing them with a quality experience, an excursion into a new world.

Think of it that way. That when you write a novel, you get to create a whole new world. And place it between two covers.
That's powerful.

To become masterful at it, you have to keep learning, keep investing in your own mind. The best writers never stop learning and exploring. Continuous learning is essential to the ability to create quality experiences for your readers.

Also, know that the best writers never "arrive."

In becoming a masterful writer, understand that your quest will be an ongoing and never-ending journey toward a nebulous pinnacle. Your journey is not simply about arriving at a particular destination, but it's about the people you connect with in your travels and the lessons you learn about life all along the way.

Understand that your total satisfaction with anything you write will be elusive. There's no magical moment of completion in which you achieve the perfect manuscript. You may always find a little room for improvement, even after your work has gone to press, always one more phrase you could have worded differently, or a character you could have expanded or eliminated. There may always be one typo that edges past the most critical scrutiny. But at some point, you'll just realize … it's done. That for the moment, you have written all you can write. You've told the best story you can tell in the most effective way you can tell it. You make yourself stop tweaking it. And you publish.

Reid Hoffman, founder of LinkedIn said, *"If you are not embarrassed by the first version of your product, you've launched too late."*
This statement can be applied to your writing as well. In other words, don't tweak your novel ad infinitum, seeking perfection. Get it in the most presentable and professionally edited format you can, and publish! Learn from your reviews. You can always make revisions and release a new and improved version later.

To be a masterful writer, you must write for the sheer joy of it. For the opportunity to share with others and enlighten their minds. For the opportunity to have interesting conversations and learn from them. Write with honesty and depth of feeling and character. Go beyond the surface and unearth what lies beneath. Go to the core. Get to the heart.

Don't settle. Don't get complacent. Don't neglect practical experience.

Keep exploring. Keep learning. Keep discovering. Keep reading other's writing. Listen to other's writing.

And just keep writing. Every day.

There's a novel inside of you. Let's get it into print.

Part 1: Your Journey Begins.

Chapter 1. About This Book.

You really can finish your novel in 90 days or less. It will take focus, discipline, determination, and dedication.

But ask yourself an important question before you begin. Ask yourself *why* you want to write your novel in 90 days.

If it's because you want to manifest the discipline of writing every day and of writing with purpose and an objective in mind, then yes, you should proceed. If it's because you're driven to write and you want to push yourself to a new level, then yes, by all means proceed. Impetus is a good thing.

But whatever time limit you set, make sure you enjoy the journey and learn new things along the way. Make sure that your focus is on the quality of the experience, for you the writer as well as the reader, and not the dollars that may or may not come at the other end. Between rushing through your writing project just to get it done and taking too long to complete it while striving for perfection ... there is a happy medium. It's probably a very fine line. Seek it carefully or you will miss it.

Take this as your opportunity to be creative in creating a *learning process.*

And when it comes to creativity, I don't like too many rules. Rules can be so ... binding. Rules about writing can keep you within a conventional framework, perhaps steering you toward conventional work. I'm inviting you here to explore. I'm asking you to go deeper.

I want you to see you ... *do you.*

For example, when I offer jewelry classes, I don't take a formulaic approach. I never have the participants all start with the exact same materials and require them to make a piece that as closely as possible replicates my sample. Instead, the sample I show them is to provide an example of where they *can* go with the project, not where they *should* go or *must* go. Each participant selects and brings to class her own focal element, be it an interesting bead or gemstone, even something unrelated to jewelry like an antique key or some intriguing hardware component or antique store find. Everyone in the class makes something different. I demonstrate techniques and then set them free to apply the techniques in the way *they* want to use them. At the end of the class, everyone has created a unique piece. No one is disappointed that their finished piece didn't turn out *exactly* like mine. Each has learned the techniques, but each has applied her own "hand."

So this book, Masterful Novel Writing, is not an "instruction manual" per se. It does not contain a prescriptive, step by step procedure for composing a novel with rules and prepared checklists. If that's what you're looking for, you won't find that in this book. But I hope you'll read on for the process insights I will share and the words of encouragement. When it comes to novel and short story writing, mine is a more freeform approach. You will get to apply your own hand, the same way that I approach making art jewelry. Think of the novel writing process I will describe as more like ... creating an itinerary for a journey ... and then embarking, *maybe without every reservation confirmed.*

Now, I don't know your schedule and other obligations, or even how committed you really are to writing your novel. I'm just here to help you get started and to show you how to build your story in a less regimented way, to share some good food for thought. So here's how you can best use this guide:

Read it through in its entirety before you begin your novel. This will give you a comprehensive idea of what is involved in the journey to completion of a manuscript. Then read the book again, build your itinerary, add references and reminders from the topics covered in this guide, and assign completion dates to the sections – as best you can, in the way that works best for you. You may wish to use storyboarding software or a spreadsheet to complete this process. If you're a visual organizer, you may enjoy building a series of interconnected mind maps or using a project management app. I roll with a spiral notebook and a pen and build a (usually very messy) handwritten itinerary. In fact, all of my writings and graphic designs begin with a chicken scratch outline with research notes or a rough sketch to lay out my path and fix the general direction in my mind.

Once you've developed your itinerary, you'll review it for missing transitions, smoothness of flow, character appearances.
You'll discover: 1) who is going on the journey with you, 2) what places the journey will take you, and most importantly, 3) what problems you and your travelers will encounter and how you will resolve them.

Day 1 begins with finding inspiration and developing your book idea. You'll end with completing your manuscript on Day 70 and can use the last two sets of 10 days for professional editing/typesetting/final cover creation and pre-press preparation for publishing. Or you can push the writing process out to the full 90 days. Your choice.

But you can do this.

Now let's talk about where and how to find the words.

Chapter 2. Finding the Words.

Therein lies the biggest challenge of all in writing a novel: Finding the words.
Where do you even start?

That's the reason why most people give up on this, even before they begin. It's not easy, way more than challenging to put thoughts into words and have those words deliver the impact that you anticipated. It's hard to know what to write first and what you will write next and how in the world you will ever bring this thing to fruition.

Here's what you need to know, understand, and accept in order to begin: If it feels impossible, it's because you are making some unfair presumptions. You may not even realize you're doing it.

Here's what I mean. When you sit down at your keypad or your desk to write a novel, you find yourself looking down a very long and winding road into a distant fog. You're seeing an endless stretch of yet to be written words that form a story you've decided must be EPIC by the time it concludes.
Yes you are. Admit it.

Everyone wants what they write to be EPIC.

And you're thinking about all the great and famous works you have read, the books that have won Pulitzers and Nobel Peace Prizes and other prestigious awards. You're thinking about pieces written by Poet Laureates and celebrity screenwriters and authors whose every release lives on the New York Times Best Sellers list for months. You're thinking that whatever you write has to measure up to that standard ... or be deemed unworthy. And that you will perhaps be vilified unmercifully for having the audacity to write something and publish it. Admit that too.

Maybe you're hearing the voice of a significant person in your life, someone whose opinion really matters to you, telling you you're not going to be any good at this. Telling you you're not any good at anything. Envious that you're always good at everything. Maybe it's the critical voice of someone long gone from your present, still haunting you from the past.

Maybe it's your own critical spirit denigrating your desire and confidence.

Maybe you're thinking about what I said at the start of this book, that you must provide a quality experience for your reader and you're wondering if you can come anywhere close to that.

Read what I said again: *The key to masterful writing is developing your ability to create a quality experience for your reader.*

The operative word there is *developing*. It says *developing your ability*. That means becoming masterful is an ongoing process. No one expects you to write the epic novel your first time out. In order to let the words flow that you have inside, you have to remove that mindset, get from behind those negative voices. That belief that, somehow, you're not going to measure up to some lofty standard you're unreasonably imposing on yourself ... or that you're allowing someone else to impose.

Secondly, my opening statement said *your reader*. Not *every* reader.

No one in the history of humanity has written *anything* that resonates with EVERYONE. The most widely published and distributed book in history is the Bible. Yet look at the vast array of belief and opinion that exists regarding its content.

Don't set yourself up for the impossible and then be disappointed when you don't accomplish ... the impossible.

Yes, of course you should do the best writing you can. Yes, you should absolutely not just put any old thing out there.

But no, you should NOT decide that you're not going to measure up.

Truth be told, even the "best" writers are often insecure about their work. Many wonder, even after a string of successes, will *this one* be the novel that bombs?

It's a weird psychological phenomenon that 100 people can tell you you're brilliant, shower you with accolades, proclaim to the hilltops how much they've learned from you, how deeply your message resonated with them. They can all be on their feet, standing in ovation, cheering and shouting your name. And your eyes come to rest on the one person three rows back who is still seated, arms folded, face shrouded in negativity, and suddenly that's all you remember. Suddenly it's all about the one angry face of someone who is *not your reader.*

Writing really is a vulnerable endeavor. It's the wearing of your faintest heart on your sleeve. Until you face that down, you won't be able to find your story and write your novel. Until you clear your mind, you won't be able to set sail and enjoy the journey.

In order to get started, you need to kick all those naysayers off your boat, right away. That includes your own self-deprecating spirit.

You'll find your opening words by letting yourself off the hook. Stop thinking about how people will respond. Stop imagining the review comments. None of that matters right now. Just focus on the process and let your words flow until you get your draft written. Then you can go back and retool, rethink, refine.

Letting yourself off the hook is the secret behind getting those first words down ... and moving toward writing mastery.

Now. Are you ready?

Chapter 3. Inspiration.

OK, so here we are. Naysayers shut down. Mind clear.
What are you going to write about?

Starting a novel can be a daunting task. Kinda scary. You open a blank document on your word processing screen – or open a journal to page one if you prefer pad and pen – and then you stare at its emptiness. Your mind goes blank. All the words you thought you had inside have suddenly vanished.

Intimidating, right?

But don't give up yet. Throw down the gauntlet and tell Intimidation you're about to crush this.

Let's start with an understanding. What is a novel?

Here's my interpretation: A novel is simply a story of characters and complexity, told in a unique and compelling way, *novel* in that it's different than any other story. Like a *novel* idea.

And that's exactly how a novel starts – with an idea. One intriguing inspiration. Or perhaps two that can be realistically and seamlessly joined together. For your novel, you will need a believable main character that your reader can love and a main secondary character to create opposition of some kind, and that possibly, your reader can hate. And you will need a "situation" – an issue, problem, challenge, or conflict that will resolve at the conclusion. To put it simply, you need a story that you can tell with vivid pictures and realistic characters and an interesting problem to solve.

If you already have an idea for your novel or have already gotten your book started, great! But read on ... You may discover you need to start anew.

Maybe you don't have an idea. Nothing fully fleshed out yet. Maybe you just know there's a story you could write ... somewhere inside you ... if only you could figure out how to begin.

We can find your story. Let's look around for some inspiration.

Many books on writing tell you to write what you know. And that advice has some true merit. The easiest path is to sit down and write within your area of expertise, and yes, you are expert at something. Look in your mirror. What has your life experience involved?

Maybe you're an expert at gardening. How could you tie that into a story? Maybe you're an engineer or an architect or a teacher or a musician. What kind of story could be built around a character who has a passion for ... the cello? Maybe you're a museum tour guide or a really great cook. Maybe you've lived in another country. What cultural observations did you make that moved you beyond stereotypes and enlightened you?

Maybe you're the survivor of a crime or a catastrophic illness. How can your experience inform a story?

Or maybe you're an expert at surviving in a dysfunctional family. Imagine the characters and storylines you could develop with a little creative embellishment on experience. (Just be careful of character assassination – you don't want to get sued!)

So write about what you know? Ok, maybe that's a good place to start.

But consider this. In writing about what you know, it will be easier for you to assume that others know what you know. Sometimes when you're the expert, you may take others' knowledge for granted and assume that what's clear to you is clear to them. Or you assume they don't know anything at all and suddenly your novel is sounding like school. That can result in an unintentionally condescending tone – a talking down to your readers.

In writing about what you know, perhaps you won't be as inclined to ask questions. The deep probing questions that go way beyond the surface, in search of the deeper story.

Maybe you'll learn more and have more to offer by writing about what you *don't* know.

If you want to build your novel around an architect and don't know anything about the field of architecture, go do some homework. Maybe your story takes place in a rural villa in South Florida. Research that region thoroughly. Go there! Conduct some interviews. Read some travel blogs. Study the different occupations within the architecture field. Maybe your character loves the outdoors as well – how about making your character a landscape architect?

What if your landscaper digs something up in a customer's yard that was never supposed to be found? And what if a competing landscape company was involved in burying it ...?

Generate ideas for your story by asking questions. What did the landscaper dig up? Who buried it? Who else knew about it? What if ...? Or suppose ...?

Or pick up a magazine and choose a compelling picture. Who is the main person in that photo? What is happening in the scene? What might the person be thinking? Where is the action taking place? A foreign country? A place you've been? Maybe there's a secondary person looking on in that photo. How could that character add interest to the mix? What's happening behind the scenes in their lives?

Go grab a coffee in your favorite shop and take a seat. People-watch for a while. Observe people interacting with each other. This can be fascinating. Take a notepad along and make some notes. Jot down descriptions of people – what they're wearing, how they move through the space. Are other people reacting to them? How? What are people talking about? Can you hear their conversations? Look at that couple over there, sitting together but always looking away from each other. Are they meeting for the first time? Angry with each other? Ill-matched? Disappointed? What kind of story could they live out in your novel?

Ideas are everywhere. You don't have to tax your brain to come up with a compelling storyline.

All you have to do is ask some probing questions. Look at a scene or a painting or a situation ... and then go deeper. What lies beneath the surface? What undercover story is waiting to be told?

Doesn't matter if the idea you come up with has already been done. The Book of Ecclesiastes says there's nothing new under the sun. Everything has been done already. So just go for it and write *your* story in *your* voice.

Look at the romance genre, for example. The formula is always the same: characters meet; strife ensues; love triumphs. Predictable, yet romance readers can't get enough – because every one of those stories carries with it the individual hand of its writer, the crafting of a quality experience for the readers who love the genre.

Your job is complex, yet amazingly simple. You just have to tell your story in your own individual and nonpareil way. You just have to bring a fresh perspective to the idea you select.

Explore and decide, in a broad overview, who you're going to write about and what's going to happen. Take a couple of days to do that. Find your story. We'll flesh out the details in the sections to come.

Chapter 4. Living in Your Head.

Novel writers walk around with characters living in their heads. These characters, whether in sharp or nebulous form, materialize in the writers' imaginations and begin sharing tidbits from their story.

Now that you've determined the broad context of your story, you'll find that characters will begin to show up and reveal themselves to you, one or two at a time. Not necessarily in order of their appearance on your stage. Some will play central roles and others, minor roles.

As the story develops, you may even discover that some of these characters living in your head are misplaced – not even meant for this particular story. But don't banish them away forever. They may have an essential role to play in your next novel.

And yes, if you have one novel inside, then you do have another. Or two. Or more!

Store what you know about these misplaced characters in an archive document until their time comes. Use a notes app or create a physical document or spreadsheet for this, or go low tech and create an index card deck. When it comes to creativity, sometimes tactile is better than digital.

Start paying attention to the characters who speak and the information they are sharing with you. I know this may sound a little crazy. But yes, they will actually begin to communicate with you ... if you let them.

Study each character that is developing in your mind. Ask questions about the character's life and experience. Hone in on personality and demeanor.

Because it's important that your characters be realistic. Your readers will want to understand them, relate to them, feel some kind of connection to them, even if that feeling is dislike. But remember, in a success formula, you really don't want your main character to be disliked. The main character has to appeal to your audience. Your reader wants the main character to "win." Otherwise, the story may become tedious and frustrating in its negative perspective and not-soon-enough comeuppance. When a negative character wins, it can feel so wrong. The story doesn't quite satisfy.

(Though when a negative character wins, that usually means there's a sequel coming ...)

Let your characters tell you who they are and why they exist.

For example, why is the competing landscape architect so determined to drive your main character out of business? Is it purely greed and obsessive ambition? Or could there be more to it? Perhaps you now meet a third character hovering just off-stage in the shadows, the ex-spouse of the main character, now (unhappily?) married to the competitor. What new information does the ex-spouse bring to the table?

See how the story begins to reveal itself as characters appear and tell you who they are?

But when new characters appear, they should be there for a specific reason. We'll talk about that more in Part 2.

Sometimes your characters will tell you things that make absolutely no sense to you – at first. But then you'll realize that they've given you more clues to the storyline.

Ask them for the details and listen carefully. Then figure out how all the information fits. Don't force a character into a mold that isn't right for the story – just because it seems like a good idea at the time. Be willing to release what's not working. Characters can provide misinformation – if they're in the wrong story.

Part of the joy of writing a novel is figuring out the journey from Situation A to Conclusion B, otherwise known as your plotline. Think of novel writing as solving a puzzle, or deciphering a riddle. You've got a cast of characters, some events, a locale or two, a period of time, and a conflict to resolve by the end of the story. What happens and how does it end? The answers are right there, hiding in plain sight. You just have to find the most interesting and descriptively entertaining journey to reaching the conclusion. Tell *that* story.

A fun way to build characters is to cast celebrity actors into their roles. If your novel were to be made into a movie, who would ideally play those parts? Hold an open casting in your mind and select actors to take the roles in your story. This can help you visualize your characters and make them real for your readers – even though they may substitute actors of their own as they read your book. The idea is to make your characters real and to give them depth and interest. Like avatars, when you know what your characters look like, you can describe their facial expressions and body language in richer detail. You begin to see more clearly through your imagination.

Keep in mind as you tell your story that if your reader doesn't care about your characters, they may not even finish the book. And that's the whole point of writing a novel – to get your reader engaged enough and invested enough to stay with you until the satisfying conclusion of the story. That quality experience is what makes novels such a joyful pastime for those who love reading.

Chapter 5. Travel Plans.

So far, you've developed a broad overview of what will take place in your story, how it will begin and how it ends, and you have clarified the main characters with an understanding of the tension that motivates them.

Now it's time to work out some more of your itinerary details before you begin writing.

Note: *You may already have seen an important moment in your book, the very scene that started you on this novel journey. You know the scene I mean. The one that keeps recurring in your mind.*

Maybe you saw your main character emerge from the trees and stop tentatively beside a rural route, battered knapsack hanging from her shoulder, a frail child at her feet, clutching her hand and looking up with apprehension. Maybe you felt the gnawing pull of their empty stomachs. Maybe you heard the truck rumble to a stop beside them and a deep baritone from within, commanding them to get in.

Perhaps you have already written a few paragraphs or even a few pages and captured that scene. Your novel has already begun. That's ok – you needed to get that down while it was flowing. It's probably pivotal in your story.

That said, I still want you to stop now and create an itinerary, a plan that incorporates and builds upon what you've already composed, so that you will have clear sense of direction going forward.

Many a masterful writer writes from a plan, for novels and other fiction as well as non-fiction writing. Developing a plan creates a foundation for your story, lining up the sequence of events that drive Situation A to Conclusion B. This may be the hardest part of the process but is a most essential step.

Not everyone likes to travel with a planned itinerary. Maybe you just like to board a mode of transportation and see where you end up. You may feel the writing and development process should be more free-flowing and just happen organically. That may work for some writers but ...

You've heard of writers who took 20 years to finish a novel? Very likely many of them were writing in the organic blind – no outline or clear sense of direction or in-depth knowledge of their characters. Or they've just spent the last 20 years tweaking their poor books to death. Waiting for their magical muses to show up and grant them the perfect words.

You can wander aimlessly for an eternity trying to journey through a story without a GPS.

Also, when you write in the blind, you can easily write yourself into a corner and discover there's no way out. Your story can come to a full stop, miles short of Conclusion B and no viable way to get there.

So I suggest having a travel plan, even if it's only a rough sketch of the storyline, to guide you along the path and keep loose ends from developing and misplaced characters from appearing onstage.

Begin your itinerary by inserting the beginning of your story (Situation A) at the top and how your story will end (Conclusion B) at the bottom and the build the sequential path between the two from start to finish. Include as little or as much detail as you need to help you keep your writing on track.

You may want to write your story in parts that cover specific spans of time. For example, part one may include what's happening in the present, part two may go back in time and share some history, and part three may join the previous two together and move on to the final outcome. That's a format I like but you use whatever story format tells your story best.

You may want to include some strategic literary devices such as flashbacks or foreshadowing to tie your timeframes together and add interest and intrigue to the storyline. (Just be careful not to use these devices too often as they may create confusion for the reader.)

Defining your sequence of events will help you work out any problematic details in your storyline. For example, if the beginning of your story takes place in New York City but ends up in the Everglades, your itinerary should indicate how the transition of locale takes place. Major changes like that should always make sense for the story and not occur in a convoluted way that will seem unrealistic to the reader.

Review your tentative plan for loose ends, smoothness of flow, character appearances. Tentative, because things are always subject to change. Once you have a good working plan, assign completion dates to each chapter or section. Day 1 begins with researching your book idea. End with completing your manuscript on Day 70 and use the last two sets of 10 days for professional editing/final cover creation and pre-press preparation for publishing.

Set a goal to write 2222 words a day. Oh ... That sounds like a rule, doesn't it?

But the goal is to get you focused on writing every day and putting forth a concerted effort. After 90 days, the habit of writing will be ingrained ... maybe even the *need* to write every day. And you will find that you're writing faster and you're writing better. Push yourself to make the quota each day.

Do the math – in 70 days, you'll have written 155,000+ words with 20 days left to review and prep for publication. Push it to the full 90 days and you'll have a novel of 200,000 words.

Once you have your sequence of events mapped out and you're spending quality time writing, more scenes will begin to come alive in your mind.

Are you getting excited about your novel? I hope so! Before you start writing, remember to finish reading this guide in its entirety so you'll understand the process to come and the important considerations to keep in mind as you develop your story!

Next, there are some preliminary categories you should recognize. Let's talk about genres.

Chapter 6. Learn Genre Rules.

Fiction writing includes a number of specific genres that each have their own definitions and rules. You may find it useful, if you're not already familiar with these categories, to read some books in each type and figure out which genre incorporates your style of writing. Note also, that many of these have been combined into hybrids in recent years – combinations of one or more genres, creating multiple avenues of appeal for your writing. It's really an exciting time to be in the publishing world!

Some of the most common genre categories include the following:

Mainstream. These are novels written in everyday language, usually long and printed in large qualities, often written by best-selling authors with widely recognized names. Think Danielle Steel and John Grisham.

Literary. This genre features writing that is lyrical, poetic, and artistically descriptive. Literary fiction is more focused on the quality of language and expression than the action taking place. Books in this genre may be experimental and challenge conventional structures.

Young Adult. Also referred to as "YA," these are novels written for an audience of readers in the 12 to 17 age group.

Thriller. Thrillers are written to evoke a sense of danger, excitement and suspense complete with good guy heroes and bad-guy criminals, espionage, law enforcement, and illegal activities.

Romance. Exactly what the name says, a romance novel tells the story of a love relationship between a man and woman and follows a very specific formula. Romances include a lot of drama, may take place in interesting and exotic locales, and involve fluctuating conflicts that threaten to destroy the relationship. But in the end, there is always reconciliation and a happy ending. Harlequin says it all.

Ethnic. Fiction written for and about a particular ethnic group or culture such as African-American, Jewish, Asian, Native American, or another specific group, often involving conflict between the characters' cultural expectations and those of the national society in which they live.

Western. Stories that take place in the Old West of the 1700's and 1800's. Think of the old Western series and movies you've seen on television. The tough hero faces struggle, danger, and harsh conditions on the frontier but beats the odds and overcomes in the end.

Horror. Horror fiction that focuses on creating a sense of fear and foreboding for the reader. Stephen King books should come to mind in this category.

Fantasy. Fantasy fiction that takes place in imaginary worlds with altered realities.

Science Fiction. Often paired with Fantasy, science fiction stories deal with futuristic elements that might actually be possible (while Fantasy is not likely to ever happen).

Hybrid categories, as explained, combine popular genres. Examples may include combinations such as Science Fiction/Horror or Ethnic/Romance/Thriller. The genre list above is not complete – there are many more categories of writing. You'll have to do some research to find your fit. Knowing your genre will be key when it comes to finding publishers, agents, reviewers, and marketing venues for your book.

Just understand that each genre has its own rules and formulas. Book reviewers, bloggers, and readers know and recognize their favorite styles and will be quick to let you know if you have incorrectly categorized your book.

Understanding the genre in which you're writing will help you tell your story.

Chapter 7. Dialogue and Grammar.

Dialogue is the conversation that takes place in your novel.
Dialogue is a key element of any good story – whether it's the continuing stream of inner thoughts that your narrator shares with the reader or the spoken conversations that take place between characters. Your characters will have to speak to convey information and to let the reader know what they are thinking and feeling.

Dialogue can also involve the exchange of nonverbals – gestures and body language.

Additionally, characters' conversations should sometimes be a little cryptic – in that the reader has to read "between the lines" to match up what's being said with the gestures described. One character may respond with "I'm OK," with arms folded and lips tight, while another says "I'm OK," while trembling and nervously glancing around. These two responses paint completely different pictures in your reader's mind. The reader will "hear" each of those "I'm Ok" responses differently.

Write your dialogue in the way people normally speak. Language is generally not so formal these days, even in business writing, unless it's an academic or scientific treatise. Use contractions like *I'd* and *she'll* instead of *I would* and *she will* to cut back on formality and make conversations sound more natural.

As you write conversations, read your exchanges aloud to ensure they sound natural. If you find yourself stumbling through the dialogue, make changes until it reads comfortably. If you are not writing in your first language, be sure to have a native speaker edit your dialogue. Awkward conversation can be frustrating for your reader. However, you may use awkward language with intention, if that's how the character would speak.

Your dialogue should immerse the reader into the story so there's a sense the reader is right there, present on the scene. Poor dialogue will stop the flow and yank the reader out of the story, focusing attention on the language itself rather than the story action.

For ideas on structuring dialogue, listen to movies and dramatic television programs. Notice how people just speak naturally? Their conversations are not stilted and don't sound rehearsed or like they're reading directly from an unfamiliar script. That's what you want to strive for in your dialogue.

Now. All that said, where does grammar fit in?

Good grammar is essential for the prose that falls between conversations. Poor grammar, no matter how riveting the story, can be a distraction and pull down the intrinsic value of what you have written.

If you're not good at grammar, take steps to review and build your skillset. Kids manage to get all the way through high school and sometimes even college with only a rudimentary knowledge of grammar rules, punctuation, and spelling. And now with text messaging? SMH. Don't depend on your word processing program to recognize every error. Final editing and proofreading still requires a human eye.

Subject-verb agreement is an important area of focus when improving your grammar. Learn to keep your verb tenses parallel and use subjective and objective pronouns correctly. For example:

Incorrect: For years, they kept the secret from he and I.
Correct: For years, they kept the secret from him and me.

Incorrect: If I would have known about it, I would have came to your party.
Incorrect: If I would of known about it, I would of come to your party.
Correct: If I had known about it, I would have come to your party.

Did you think the incorrect statements were the correct ones? Better go and do some grammar review!

Keep in mind that poor grammar will diminish the perceived quality of your book and poor dialogue will make it a tiresome read. If you have trouble in these areas, don't let it stop you from writing your novel. Just get your words down into a manuscript and later, hire a professional editor to help you correct the errors.

Chapter 8. Who Said That?

Another important consideration for writing your novel is to decide whose point of view (POV) will govern the story. There are a few options open to you, variations on first person and third person.

First Person. First person means the story is narrated using "I." This perspective can give a dramatic immediacy to the story, placing the reader right in the heart of the action and privy to all the narrator's thoughts and feelings. Keep in mind a couple of caveats, though, with the first person POV: 1) Your writing will be restricted to sharing information with your reader that only the narrator would know. You can't suddenly switch and start revealing other characters' thoughts. 2) Writing in first person POV leads the reader to believe it's actually you, telling your own personal story. So if your narrator is abused, or abusive, assaulted, deals with an illness, whatever – the readers will unconsciously believe that situation happened to you. Just some food for thought to consider regarding the first person POV.

Third Person. This POV uses s/he and him/her but still tells the story from one character's point of view. You will have to be careful to hold the information shared in the story to that which the character would realistically know.

Omniscient. Omniscient means "all knowing." The omniscient POV gives you the freedom to share whatever information you want to move your story along. You can write from any character's POV. You can switch POVs from one section to the next. You can strategically withhold information to create some suspense or build drama in your story. This is probably the easiest and least restrictive POV in which to write.

Second Person. The second person POV addresses "you" directly and is rarely used in fiction novels. This POV is more suitable for creative non-fiction or instructional writing such as this novel writing guide which is written for you. You can surprise your reader, on few and select occasions, by allowing the narrator of a passage to suddenly speak directly to the reader.

Select one POV and stick with it. Inconsistency in POV can become get confusing for your reader. When you get to the editing stage of your writing process, POV will be an important perspective to monitor for consistency.

Chapter 9. Finally, the Finale.

It's important to have some idea how your story will end before you start writing. Knowing the grand finale, the climactic conclusion of the story, will give you a sense of focus and direction as you write and keep you from, as we discussed earlier, writing yourself into a corner.

That said, the characters may show you that they have a different story to tell and a different outcome in mind. You may find that you'll have to alter your plans, move some things around in your itinerary, or eliminate certain events or characters altogether.

When you decide to eliminate a character, a section you have written, or other material from your draft, move it to a separate book addendum file and hold onto it. If things change and you decide that material or character is needed, you'll be glad you saved it. No need for you to learn that lesson the hard way! Even if you end up completely rewriting the saved section, you will at least have a starting point and not have to lament over thinking you deleted "the perfect words."

Make your goal to write through to the finale, even if you don't write in chronological order, without too much rewriting and self-editing. This will be a challenge. New plot twists may come to you as you move along and you will have to incorporate those changes.
Remember that your objective is to get through to the end and produce a solid working draft – so don't keep self-editing. Don't spend hours or days tweaking one scene. Steer clear of the path that leads to 20 years.

Chapter 10. Write Every Day.

Writing is a craft. Just like playing an instrument or mastering any other art form, writing takes disciplined application and practice. It's a totally hands-on endeavor.

You can become a masterful writer if you write every day. Write something. Every day. That doesn't mean **brain-scribing** either. That means make a commitment. Low tech pen to paper, fingers to keyboard, or high tech stylus to keypad, but make the commitment to write every day.

You can even dictate your writing into a word processing program if you're not a fast typist. No excuse if you've got a broken finger or sprained wrist. You can still "write."

Note: I remember procrastinating about my writing once. Feeling uninspired to get started. Feeling pinned down and trapped beneath the dreaded "writer's block." (I've since come to believe there's no such thing as writer's block.) I was watching a movie about Gabriela Brimmer, a writer who had cerebral palsy. Born in 1947 Mexico, she began her writing as a teen, years before word processing software, using a typewriter. She didn't have the use of her arms and hands – she could only strike the typewriter keys with the toe of one foot. Imagine the sheer strength of will and determination you would have to muster up to write your entire novel with one toe, one letter of one word at a time. But she did it. She finished it. And then went on to write more.

We have it so easy. The majority of you reading this have the use of both hands. We have word processing and voice recognition software. Don't lose your writing momentum to lame excuses.

And there's really no such thing as writer's block. You may be unfocused, or waiting for organic blind magic to happen, or maybe just tired. But you're not blocked.

And even if there is such a thing ... you don't have time for that. You have a novel to write.

As William Faulkner famously stated, *"I only write when I am inspired. Fortunately, I am inspired at 9 o'clock every morning."*

Write every day and write anywhere ... perhaps even designate a special place to write. A studio or a quiet corner where your thoughts can flow uninterrupted, where you can leave and return to pick up right where you left off. Or maybe not so much a particular space as a particular time. Write early in the morning, before the kids are out of bed and the chaos of your day begins. Or late at night after everyone else has gone to sleep. Turn the television off and shut down your social networking. Get away from your usual crew at work sometimes and write during your lunch hour.

Words will come to you at the oddest times. Keep a notepad with you or speak into a recording device so you can capture your thoughts while they're flowing. Don't assume you will recall those words later exactly as they came to you. Most likely, you will not.

Stick to your goal to write 2222 words a day. Push yourself to make your quota. Make up for any lost time or shortfalls from the previous day. In 70 days, you'll have written 155,000 words. In 90 days, 200,000 words. And when you finish your novel ... keep writing every day. By the time you finish, the next story will be forming.

Don't sit around waiting for your muse to come and sweep you off to your writing space and pour out brilliance from your fingertips into the keyboard. Don't rely on random inspiration to show up on impulse and feed you magic words. Don't allow yourself to get caught up in that no-man's land of imaginary writers' block.

Make your writing process a discipline, with your goal clearly marked ahead of you.

See the finish line in the distance?

Pace yourself, like a distance runner, so you can stay the course until you cross that finish line, with enough strength in reserve for that final burst of speed. Lean into that tape.

That's what I'm doing as I write this book. I'm seeing it in print, in your hands or digitally presented on your screen. Helping to guide and fortify you to write your novel.

If you're reading this now, I crossed that finish line.

Part 2: The Middle Passage.

Chapter 11. Deadline. No Deadline.

Writing your novel will take as long as you say it will take. Writing this one in 90 days is just a number chosen to reach 200,000 words. If you think it will take you two years to finish your novel, it will. If you believe you can finish it in six months, you can. It's a self-fulfilling prophecy.

Whatever time allowance you give yourself is the amount of time you'll need ... But don't allow lame excuses to alter your schedule.

Have you ever noticed how your lifestyle swells to the limit of the budget you're working with? Time works the same way. Your writing tasks will swell to fill the amount of time you have allotted to them.

Don't take 20 years to write your novel.

Give yourself a deadline. Decide when you begin how long it's going to take you to compose your first draft and what you're going to accomplish from week to week and day to day. Stick to that schedule. Don't let anything unnecessary get in the way of the schedule you have planned. A freeform approach to writing doesn't necessarily mean be undisciplined.

Create realistic milestones and commit them to a calendar, preferably a digital one or an app that will send you reminders, help you gauge progress, and keep you on track.

Set realistic milestones – you know what your days entail. You know the real demands on your time. You know what's beyond your control. Plan accordingly. Work rest breaks into your schedule. Make time to walk away from your novel for a day and come back to it with fresh eyes.

If you get a little stuck, stop and read the work of a writer you love for an hour or two. Listen to some authors talk about their work online or in a podcast. Your creativity will kick in again and be ready to roll when you get back to your writing.

But set a schedule and stick to it.

Because the truth is, especially if you're a first-time author, *there really is no deadline*. Unless you're under contract, nothing really bad is going to happen if you take a few days, weeks, or months longer to finish your novel. Life will be happening to you and around you the whole time you're writing it. Circumstances will arise. Other commitments will take precedence. People you love will distract you. Email and social networking will be vying for your attention. Your favorite television series will get more exciting.

Maybe you can even see the refrigerator from your desk. Something in there will keep calling to you.

Just stay your course and go for a personal best. Cross that finish line.

Set a record. But don't sacrifice quality.

Chapter 12. See It On the Shelf.

For your novel to reach completion, visualize it now, already in the lineup, on display in your favorite bookstore. See people looking at it. Picking it up and buying it. See your cover and title on Amazon's list of Top 10 Best Sellers. See it at the top of the New York Times Best Sellers List. Believe it's going to get there. Imagine how that will feel. Think about all the thousands of books being published and see yours rising to the top of your category. Imagine it rising to the top of all categories.

That means you have to finish it. A novel that never gets written never makes a best sellers list.

So you have to finish your novel.

Writing a novel may still seem like an overwhelming and impossible task. You may wonder if you'll ever be able to complete the story. Most people give up before they ever get there. But make up your mind. Set your goal.

And don't you give up.

Just keep seeing the completed book on the shelf. You may want to get your cover done in advance, or at least a draft cover with a working title, and have it visible as an inspiration piece to encourage you as you write.

There's something inspiring about seeing the cover with your (working) title and your name on the front. Becoming an author is an awesome accomplishment.

You want to know what that feels like. Don't you?

Make the commitment. Finish your book.

There it is, on the shelf. Wow. You did it ... Can you see it?

Chapter 13. Page 1 Chokehold.

One of my favorite writers was Sidney Sheldon. I never forgot the opening words of his thriller, *If Tomorrow Comes* (Copyright 1985), which read as follows: *"She undressed slowly, dreamily, and when she was naked, she selected a bright red negligee to wear so that the blood would not show."*

Now *that* is what I call a Page 1 Chokehold.

That's how you grab your reader at the very opening of your story.

Then you just hold on, relax sometimes, release the tension, but you never, ever let go. You keep your reader engaged with you until the last page of the journey.

Some novels seem to meander around for a number of pages or even chapters before anything really interesting or exciting happens. Determined readers will doggedly read on, especially if they love the writer, giving the author a chance to get things going.

Remember that literary fiction is not characterized by high drama and a riveting plotline. The literary genre is about the crafting of beautiful language so there may be long and eloquently written passages but not a lot of action. Fans of this genre just love the experience of the writer's choice of words.

Readers who prefer more instant gratification may give up before they get to the really good part.

Keep this in mind as you write your story. There are certain genre rules you may have to follow and certain expectations you will have to satisfy, as you learned in your research. Be true to the genre you have chosen. Know and understand the rules and techniques of the craft so that you can determine which ones to bend. I believe you should write that book that's in you. Not with disregard or disrespect for rules and structure ... but finding places where you can afford to experiment. That's how you produce a book that stands apart from others.

Write the book that's really in your heart. Its audience will find it.

But just for the challenge of it, grab your reader in a chokehold on page one. The sooner you grasp your reader's attention, the better.

Chapter 14. Live. Film.

Write like it's live.

Writing a novel should engage all of your senses. You should be able to see it, hear it, smell it, taste it, feel it.

As if you're right there where the action is taking place.

When I write, I see the scenes play out in front of me and I'm the scribe, the journalist on the scene who's recording what's happening.

Immerse yourself in your story as if it's live, like it's happening right in front of you, like it's coming fresh and detailed from your current memory bank, so you can pull out the richest descriptions of the surroundings and the deepest emotions of the moment.

This helps your reader to see your story as you see it. Too nebulous, and the reader is left with a lot of construction work to do. You don't want your reader to have to labor to sense your story, on any level. Some things, yes, can and perhaps should be left to the imagination, but for the most part, I believe a story works better when the reader has a true understanding or interpretation of what you want that reader to know.

This keeps confusion to a minimum, and I believe, makes for a more satisfying read.

Your talent shines in the actual telling of the story, and not so much in the telling as in the showing. Your job is to make the descriptions come alive, whether your style is poetic and metaphorical or written in everyday language. Remember, that you're creating a quality reading experience. Even if no one will read it or enjoy it but you.

Review the scenes you have written thus far. Are you providing enough detail? Is there any pertinent information missing in action?

Can you see every scene in your mind?

Can you feel the surfaces and edges in the setting? The sun burning down or the cool of the moonlight?

Can you smell the food being prepared? The dusty odor of the neglected room? The faint wafting of cologne?

Can you hear the emotion in your characters' tones of voice?

Can you see their facial features and the fit of their garments and the expressions on their faces?

Write like it's film.

Movie scenes are rarely filmed in the order that they happen in the story. Sometimes, the first scene to be shot is the final scene and all the rest are filmed in a random sequence based on actors' and directors' schedules, availability of settings and scenery props, weather conditions, whims of producers, and any number of other details and issues that impact a shooting schedule. Many scenes wind up on the "cutting room floor."

Because the film editor has to ensure that the scenes flow as if recorded in sequential order. That means consistency in placement of props and costuming and lighting and characters.

I write like I'm making a film. Watching a movie in my mind.

A scene may suddenly play itself out in my mind that belongs halfway through Part 3 although I've only written up to the end of Part 1. But I capture it all. Even if I end up leaving it on the cutting room floor, I record it while I see it in my mind. Because that's my characters telling me what's going to happen. By recording it, I'm listening to what they have to say. When I start Part 2, I have even more information about where I'm going and how the story will conclude. I can start foreshadowing that new information earlier in my writing.

But like an editor, I have to remain consciously aware of the props, costuming, lighting, and characters, where they are and how they're set at every moment. I have to remember who died on page 87 – that character can't suddenly appear on page 214. I have to remember names. If I change a character's name after a substantial amount of writing, I must make sure I correct every recurrence of the previous name.

I believe, somewhere deep inside, I'm actually a filmmaker. I love to write this way and find it most satisfying. I enjoy the challenge of creating the disparate scenes in no particular order and the craft of assembling the story. But that's just me.

Not saying you should or must write this way. It may be easier or more efficient or faster for you to start at the beginning and keep moving straight on through the plan you've developed, writing the scenes as you come to them. Nothing at all wrong with a totally linear approach.

Just be sure that when you see a new scene running clearly in your mind, you capture that information and find where it belongs in your story.

Keep the reader's senses in mind as you write. These impressions may be useful when it comes to **marketing** your completed book.

Chapter 15. Create Impetus.

Your storyline must move forward.

You can flash back and pick up moments in history, but by the end, your story has to have moved somewhere beyond the point where it started. There has to have been a change, a lesson learned, a resolution, even the left-open door to a sequel. Unless you're writing literary fiction with some element of experimentation, your story has to have pace and motion.

Otherwise, you may lose your audience.

People today are easily bored. Perhaps because we are so overstimulated by the media that surrounds us, the sights and sounds and activities that bombard our senses every day. We lose interest when transition to the next point is missing in action ... or takes too long loading up.

Your story needs impetus. The reader needs a compelling reason to keep turning the (digital) pages. One reason after another.

Impetus is the product of good transition. Transition is an event or action or dialogue or thought or a piece of information that begins in one scene and concludes in one of the next. Those transitions should be smooth ones – but throw in a little jolting change of pace every now and then, a surprising occurrence or an unexpected response. This keeps the story interesting. This keeps the reader's mind engaged and stimulated.

Take a moment now to review your itinerary again. Does your storyline really flow? Is your writing moving forward like you thought it would? Are there places where you need to build in a little drama or suspense?

When the reader gets to the end of the story, will there be the experience of satisfaction you're hoping for ... or vague disappointment?

Take a break and scan (don't start editing, just scan) through what you've written thus far. Is it building to a climax or ambling along aimlessly?

If it's effectively building to climax, press on.

(Though "effectively building" is a matter of opinion. Use a critical eye. Without self-deprecation.)

If your novel is wandering and feels aimless, go back and make some revisions. Do this now before you've gone too far to fix it. Before you have written yourself into a wall.

Chapter 16. Get in Touch.

The mark of a good friend is how easily you first got to know her and well you continue to know and understand each other.

By now, your reader should know and understand your main characters as well. They should be familiar people who have now taken up residence in your reader's head, welcome to stay until the end of the story – and beyond. You want your characters to be memorable. Unforgettable.

If your characters still seem shallow, spend some more time getting in touch with them. Peer deep into their inner cores and find out what else you don't know. Have you asked enough questions?
Because if you don't know your characters, neither does your reader. Perhaps your reader will resort to making assumptions that don't fit your story.

The reader wants to be able to get in touch with your characters, too. Your reader wants to understand what's happening. The reader has made an investment in buying your book and listening to your story. Create characters that offer the reward of depth and clarity.

If you're not sure, form an objective review crew and get some second opinions. (A crew which should not include the opinions of relatives, significant others or BFFs who think everything you do is brilliant.)

Allow your reader to see into the minds and hearts of your characters. You don't always have to be obvious about it. Show, don't tell, remember? Provide clues and intuitive signals through observations and actions, through thoughts and facial expressions. Flash back to telling moments in time that clarify current behavioral traits.

That's the most exciting part about writing a novel. You get to create a brand new world for your reader to explore. Get in touch with that world. Travel deep into the mines and recesses so you can paint the most vivid pictures and tell the most memorable story.

Chapter 17. Population Control.

When characters appear, they should be there for a specific reason. We mentioned this in Part 1, Characters in Your Head.
Do your mind-casting carefully and eliminate roles that really do belong on the cutting room floor. Don't include any more characters than you have to.

Also be careful when selecting names. Alliteration may become an evident problem – too many characters whose names begin with the same letter. Just happens sometimes.
Consider the meanings of names as you select them for your characters. Names can be used to convey a soft, lovely personality, like Rose, or convey the irony of a thorny persona, like Rose.

Some characters serve as Transition Assistants and production extras. They appear, help a character move from one place to another or share some important words of wisdom, and then their work is done. Give them a little personality, a worthy purpose, but not too much history, and let them quietly exit the stage.
They will remain good candidates to reappear and expand in a sequel, if you write one.

Be willing to let a character go if need be, but store that persona away in an archival file and ensure you have removed all references to that character, both direct and implied. You will eventually write the novel or story in which that character or scene belongs. Then you can introduce that character on a new stage.

But keep track of the population of characters filing through your story. Crowd control is important. You don't want so many characters that your reader can't remember who said or did what.

Chapter 18. Breaking Genre Rules.

To fit comfortably into a genre, your novel must meet its criteria.

Romance novels, for example, are very formulaic and as we discussed before, fans of romance novels love that formula. To you, the story format may feel predictable or even cliché, but to romance lovers, the flow of the story, the new characters and situation, the turns and twists of the plot, and the final outcome are the things that make reading and writing romance novels fun and entertaining.

My writing tends to have a literary edge but, personally, I enjoy a hybrid approach. I like mixing genres, a little romance here, a bit of thrill there, a few moments of suspense, a mysterious secret or two, all leading up to a satisfying ending. Maybe one loose end left that makes way for a sequel. At least one character who can pick up the storyline and run with it in the next book. That's how a series is born.

Just be sure you understand which rule and how many rules you are breaking. Too many and your book will be difficult to classify. Just enough and you may stand out as a unique new voice in the writing world.

Your choice.

Chapter 19. Get Your Facts Straight.

Another exciting component of writing a novel is conducting the research.

For believability, you really should get your facts straight. Even though you're creating a fictional world where anything can happen, your reader will know if you're exploring an area that you know nothing about. Especially if your reader happens to be an expert in that field.

For example, at the beginning we discussed making your main character a landscape architect. Landscape architecture, like any other occupational field, has its own language, techniques, procedures, jargon and technical terminology. If you just pull a few terms from an occupational guide, you may find out later that you have used those terms in an amateur way.

Use your novel development time to explore and conduct thorough research. You have the Web at your fingertips to locate reliable resources and expertise in any area you wish to incorporate. Contact bloggers, consult with your connections on LinkedIn or Facebook, and ask for assistance or interview an expert. Ask the expert to read over your passage and suggest modifications that would make the language more natural and technically correct.

To ensure accuracy of the information you include, find an advisor to check your terminology. If you're including a description of a medical procedure, find someone in the profession who can corroborate your description.

Explore the idea of setting your novel in an exotic place that you have never been. This is one of the areas where you can creatively veer away from only writing what you know. All you need to do is look up that country online, visit some travel sites and blogs, read about its people and its history, look at lots of photos, and get a feel for the locale in your mind. If you want to describe a resort in an exotic locale and you know someone who's actually stayed there, enlist that traveler to share pictures and impressions with you.

Many people write novels that take place in locations they have never visited in person. In fact, maybe most.

Writing is an adventure that allows you to travel, even if it's only in your imagination.

So don't be held back by the convention of only writing what you know. Give yourself an opportunity to learn something new as you continue on this journey toward your completed novel.

Part 3: Coming Home.

Chapter 20. Seal the Cracks, Unless ….

By this time, your novel has come a long way. You're entering the final leg of this journey. You're on your way home.

Now is the time to start reexamining what you've written thus far.

If you're like most, though, you've probably been cheating. You've already read and re-read some parts. You've already rewritten some sections and rewritten them again. And banished some characters from the stage.

But now, let's really seal up the cracks. Start at the beginning of your novel and move through it slowly. Make notes of things you need to correct. Be on the lookout for loose ends – things you started and didn't finish.

Did you bring anybody onstage who's still hanging around, wondering what to do? Did you start any minor story lines that you didn't resolve?

This is the time to seal up those cracks and close the loopholes, unless …

You're planning to write a sequel.

Sometimes when you're telling a story, you discover there's really more than one story in your original idea, a continuation or a secondary character seeking a rightful spot in the limelight.

In that case, you may want to shut all the doors but one. You may want to let a character escape through an exit left ajar and resolve that one in the next book. Or maybe you'll leave a trail of open doors as you move through from story to story. Writers can end up with many books in a series before they run out of steam or another new set of characters and ideas takes over.

Note: *I can still remember reading Carolyn Keene's Nancy Drew mystery series books as often as I could get to the library. It was always Nancy and her same group of friends but I couldn't get enough of those books. Carolyn Keene always tied up every loose end by the conclusion, but there was always the sense that another sleuthing adventure was right around the corner. Every next story had a whole new and exciting mystery to resolve. For me, that was masterful and influential writing.*

So look now for the continuity in your storyline and make sure you've covered all the necessary bases.

Chapter 21. Cut and File.

Don't be so enamored with the brilliance of your prose that you can't eliminate what doesn't edify.

Sometimes you write a really great passage. You love how those words flow. Love the picture it paints. Yet ... somehow it seems out of place in *this* story. Every time you read through that part, you get that same feeling, that it doesn't quite *belong*.

Maybe it belongs in another story.

You have to bite the bullet and take it out. But don't get rid of it completely. Store it away in your notes app or your archive document or your idea spreadsheet. When it's time comes, you'll know exactly where to find it.

By the way, have you been keeping a backup copy of your novel? If not, make one now. *Always* have a second copy somewhere on separate or removable media like a thumb drive or in cloud storage. If your computer should crash or come down with a virus or get stolen, you'll still have your work intact up to your last save.

Note: *I used to work as a systems analyst, overseeing a user help desk service, and one of the issues we dealt with most often was trying to help users restore unsaved files that crashed or became corrupt or were accidentally deleted. Sometimes there was just no remedy for them except to give them the most recent backup file from the server – yeah, the one from last Friday that didn't include any of this week's data – and leave them to start their data entry over again. Many had to learn the hard way to maintain a second copy of their work.*

After you have cut out sections and made corrections, you won't remember every little change you made. Don't create a situation where you will have to start all over.

Protect your work. Cut sections and file them. Save your manuscript twice as you go – once to your working file and once to external storage. Even if your software auto-saves every few minutes, make it a practice to manually save your work every 20 minutes or so. That way you'll never lose more than 20 minutes of writing. There's no guarantee the auto-saved version will restore properly.

Chapter 22. Switch Shoes.

As you review your novel, take your shoes off. Put on your reader's shoes. Try to read your work as if you're seeing it for the first time.

In fact, you may have to walk away from it again for a couple of days. Add this rest break into your 90-day schedule. When you've read something over and over again, your eyes grow accustomed to the text and start sliding over typos, missing words, and other errors, including the contextual ones.

Your brain has a way of "knowing what you meant" and will wax right past mistakes that will jump off the page when viewed with fresh eyes.

Be as objective as you can when reading your own work. Yes, it's hard. You'll probably be in love with your words. You won't want to acknowledge any flaws. But keep it real. Be honest with yourself. It will make for a much better novel.

Reid Hoffmann only said you should be embarrassed, not mortified.

Read select key passages out loud. Read your whole book aloud if you're up to it. In fact, consider recording your book for audio as well if you have a good narration voice. Readers love to hear books in the author's actual voice.

Reading aloud will point out awkward language and breaks in your word flow. It will also illuminate errors where you changed something in all other locations but this one instance – like a change of character's name. Or perhaps insertion of a wrong name.

Granted, you only have an assumed idea of what perceptions your reader will form when reading your book – but you can imagine enough of the reader's experience to know what to look for. What things annoy you about reading others' books? Make sure you cover your bases on those pet peeves in your own manuscript.

Chapter 23. Pro-Edit. Proof.

Once you have the final draft of your manuscript done, set it aside for another day or two. Don't look at it. Don't think about it. Tell those characters in your head to take five and let you rest up.

Work on another project. Relax with some tea. Just don't look at your book.

Then when you're ready, open your document and read it all the way through from start to finish. If you see anything minor, like a missed typo, go ahead and fix it. But at this point, you should not be doing major self-editing. You're reviewing your final draft in a last pass before it goes to professional editing.

It's always a good idea to have a professional editor read your manuscript. A professional will point out any glaring errors, sentences that don't make sense, grammar corrections, and structural inconsistencies. You may believe your grammar is fine but your editor may show you otherwise. In fact, you may want to solicit a professional edit prior to this stage, maybe the half-way point, if you're really feeling unsure as you move through your writing process. But I say go ahead and complete the draft first.

A professional editing job makes for a better quality of experience for your reader. If you can't afford an editor, you may have to rely on your own skills an instincts. But if you can, hire a good one and pay that editor what s/he's worth.

The final step is to proofread. Hire a professional for this as well, or pay the editor to do so if that service can be included.

If you have to proofread your own work, I recommend a three-pass method of reading through it once for clarity (which you've just done), then going word by word through the whole book, and the third time through, start at the last word of the last page and read backwards in small sections at a time until you reach the top of the document. This may seem tedious but it's a good way to catch typos. Your brain can't slide past errors as easily when the words are flowing backwards.

Sometimes, it's better to edit and proofread from a hard copy. Old school, yes, and a lot of paper, but for some reason, the errors seem to stand out more in hard copy than they do onscreen.

Note: *Save that hardcopy, perhaps even create a footer in the document before you print it and add a copyright notice that will appear on every page. I was once advised that the best proof of copyright is to date, package up, and mail a copy of your completed manuscript to yourself, leave the package sealed upon delivery and store it away. If there is ever a need to prove your ownership of copyright – and the onus of proof of ownership will be on you, not the alleged story thief – you will have a sealed and postmarked copy that's hopefully admissible in court. You can also go the route of actually registering your manuscript with the US Copyright Office (fee associated with this service). Don't forget to delete the footer from your final publication document.*

Chapter 24. After Effects.

Well. You've come a long way.

My goal was to get you through the writing part of your novel. How you will publish it – or whether you publish it at all – is really up to you.

As I said before, this is an awesome time to be in the writing business. You have numerous self-publishing opportunities available and venues through which you can market and sell your writing. You don't have to wait for an agent or a big publisher to choose you, but you can certainly pursue that route if traditional publishing is your desire. With Print-On-Demand (POD) capabilities, you no longer have to print a 1000 copies and ride around with stacks of them in the trunk of your car, hoping you can sell them all.

Do some research. There are excellent books already written on the self-publishing process as well as how to find an agent to represent you to big publishers. Learn about the book submission process and follow the instructions given – those are rules you must follow or your manuscript will be summarily rejected.

I'm just glad to meet a fellow writer, committed to crossing the finish line with your novel.

Hopefully your journey into novel-writing is a learning experience that will leave you changed. That will help you grow. That will bring ideas and words and meaning from within you that you didn't even know have been there all along.

Hopefully, you see a completed manuscript before you now and it feels ... exhilarating!

If you've completed your manuscript, it's probably also a little scary. Because now you have to release it. Get it typeset and send it out into the world where it will be publicized, scrutinized, analyzed, criticized, maybe even vandalized ... by people who are not necessarily concerned about your heart.

People you know are probably going to look at you funny. Prepare for that. Not because anything is wrong with you. Not because your novel isn't good. They're going to look at you funny because you've accomplished something awesome, so amazing that most people only wish they could do it ...

And now you have actually done it!

Releasing a novel, especially your first, is an exposure. An experience of a brand new kind of vulnerability. Hopefully, most who read your novel will love it or at least get it. Ok, some may not like it. That just goes with the territory. Make up your mind now not to be personally, internally wounded by anything you hear or read in a review. Take what's truly relevant and constructive from feedback you receive and use it to make your next novel even better. You have to keep learning. Don't stop writing. Remember that you're still on a journey towards mastery.

Writing a novel is one of the best and most satisfying things you will ever do.

Now take a deep breath.

It's time to get started on book two.

About the Author

Roz Swartz Williams is a professional writer,
graphic designer, and mixed media jewelry artisan,
living the creative life and loving every moment of it.
This is the first of The Masterful Writer Series,
a series of guides for those who wish to
master the craft of writing.

She is also the author of **The Mourning Chronicles,**
the first in a series on the journey to finding purpose,
and **Fleeing Aerie,** a Fiction Novel of the Year
Finalist as selected by ForeWord Magazine.

You can reach out to Roz at
www.lot21design.net or **www.nonpareil-ltd.com**
or follow her on Twitter: **@RozSW**

www.ingramcontent.com/pod-product-compliance
Lightning Source LLC
Chambersburg PA
CBHW070959290526
45795CB00005B/1702